Contractions

A pronunciation practice book

Colin Mortimer

Drawings by Daria Gan

Cambridge University Press

Cambridge

London · New York · Melbourne

Published by the Syndics of the Cambridge University Press
The Pitt Building, Trumpington Street, Cambridge CB2 1RP
Bentley House, 200 Euston Road, London NW1 2DB
32 East 57th Street, New York, NY 10022, USA
296 Beaconsfield Parade, Middle Park, Melbourne 3206, Australia

ISBN 0 521 21533 1

First published 1977

Printed in Great Britain by
Cox & Wyman Ltd
London, Fakenham and Reading

Contractions featured

page 8	**1**	US	Let's
	2	DO	D'you
	3		Don't
9	**4**		Revise Dialogues 1–3
	5	A M	I'm
10	**6**		I'm not
	7	IS	He's, John's, Jack's
	8		She's
11	**9**		It's, Who's
	10		Isn't, It's not, He's not
12	**11**	ARE	You're
13	**12**		They're
	13		We're
	14		Aren't, —'re not
14	**15**		Revise Dialogues 5–14
	16		Revise Dialogues 5–14
15	**17**	WILL	I'll, You'll
	18		He'll, She'll
16	**19**		It'll
	20		We'll, You'll, They'll
17	**21**		Won't
	22		Revise Dialogues 17–21
18	**23**		Revise Dialogues 17–21
19	**24**	HAVE	I've, You've
	25		They've, We've
	26		Haven't, —'ve not
20	**27**		He's, She's, It's
	28		Hasn't

page 21	**29**		Revise Dialogues 24–28
	30		Revise Dialogues 24–28
22	**31**	IS and HAS	—'s
	32		—'s
23	**33**	HAD	He'd, You'd
	34		I'd, She'd
24	**35**		It'd
25	**36**		We'd, You'd, They'd
	37		—'d, Hadn't
26	**38**		Revise Dialogues 33–37
27	**39**	WOULD	I'd, You'd, She'd, He'd
	40		It'd
	41		We'd, They'd
28	**42**		Wouldn't
	43		Revise Dialogues 39–42
29	**44**	HAD and WOULD	—'d
	45		Hadn't, Wouldn't
30	**46**	MODALS + HAVE	Should've, etc.
	47		Could've, etc.
31	**48**	General Revision	
	49	General Revision	
32	**50**	Conclusion	

Introduction

Most students are aware that 'contractions' such as *they're*, *we've* and *he'd* represent, in writing or print, the usual spoken form of *they are, we have* and *he had* (or *he would*). Many students, however, are not sure how such contractions should be pronounced, or lack experience in pronouncing them. This book and the accompanying recording provide opportunity for the intensive practice of the main contracted forms encountered in written texts. It consists of fifty short dialogues in which particular contractions are featured individually, in pairs, and in groups, with revision at appropriate stages.

Using the book

The pronunciation of each contraction is indicated in phonemic transcription in the headings to the dialogues. Standard works on phonetics will readily provide more detailed descriptions of the sounds of English in connected speech. *It must be emphasised, however, that the chief aid in using the book is a good model or models.*

There are many ways of using the dialogues, and variety is important. But in general it is suggested that before students practise a dialogue themselves, they should first hear it spoken by the model(s), to get a sense of the meaning and pronunciation of the whole. After this, they can work up from judicious and varied practice of individual contractions in isolation, then in phrases and longer stretches, to a fluent performance of the full dialogue in chorus, groups and pairs. Dialogues should be constantly revised, and some may usefully be memorised.

Linking contracted forms with following words

Particular care should be taken to link contracted forms smoothly and correctly with the word that immediately follows them. One pitfall to be avoided is that of 'over articulating', or exaggerating the pronunciation of a contraction at the junction with the next word. So, for example, some students tend to pronounce the *'d* in *he'd come* so deliberately that either a gap occurs between

5

he'd and *come*, or the neutral vowel intrudes, resulting in *heeder come* /hidə ˈkʌm/.

Further work

The dialogues can be used as a basis for simple oral comprehension, thereby enabling students to practise maintaining pronunciation improvements while giving some attention to *meaning*.

Sometimes questions can be framed to elicit answers retaining the contraction used in a dialogue:

> *e.g. Dialogue 20*
> Q. What do the speakers say will happen to all her anxieties and problems?
> A. They'll disappear.

Sometimes the questions can aim to elicit a change of contraction:

> Q. What did the speakers say would happen to all her anxieties and problems?
> A. They'd disappear.

The recording

The dialogues are recorded on cassette, and all of them except the revision dialogues are preceded by a *listen and repeat* section, with gaps on the tape for student repetition. In this preliminary section, the contractions to be used in the dialogue are drilled. The dialogues themselves are, of course, recorded without gaps, but teachers with a class, or students working individually, can use the pause and rewind mechanisms of their machines to play and repeat sections on which they wish to concentrate.

Paced reading: Students often find it helpful to read *along with* the tape; to do this kind of paced reading it may be advisable to turn down the volume of the tape a little.

6

Key to phonetic symbols

Vowels and diphthongs

i	*as in*	see /si/		ɜ	*as in*	fur /fɜ(r)/
ɪ	*as in*	sit /sɪt/		ə	*as in*	ago /ə`gəʊ/
e	*as in*	ten /ten/		eɪ	*as in*	page /peɪdʒ/
æ	*as in*	hat /hæt/		əʊ	*as in*	home /həʊm/
ɑ	*as in*	arm /ɑm/		ɑɪ	*as in*	five /fɑɪv/
o	*as in*	got /got/		aʊ	*as in*	now /naʊ/
ɔ	*as in*	saw /sɔ/		ɔɪ	*as in*	join /dʒɔɪn/
ʊ	*as in*	put /pʊt/		ɪə	*as in*	near /nɪə(r)/
u	*as in*	too /tu/		eə	*as in*	hair /heə(r)/
ʌ	*as in*	cup /kʌp/		ʊə	*as in*	pure /pjʊə(r)/

Consonants

p	*as in*	pen /pen/		s	*as in*	so /səʊ/
b	*as in*	bad /bæd/		z	*as in*	zoo /zu/
t	*as in*	tea /ti/		ʃ	*as in*	she /ʃi/
d	*as in*	did /dɪd/		ʒ	*as in*	vision /vɪʒn/
k	*as in*	cat /kæt/		h	*as in*	how /haʊ/
g	*as in*	get /get/		m	*as in*	man /mæn/
tʃ	*as in*	chin /tʃin/		n	*as in*	no /nəʊ/
dʒ	*as in*	June /dʒun/		ŋ	*as in*	sing /sɪŋ/
f	*as in*	fall /fɔl/		l	*as in*	leg /leg/
v	*as in*	voice /vɔɪs/		r	*as in*	red /red/
θ	*as in*	thin /θin/		j	*as in*	yes /jes/
ð	*as in*	then /ðen/		w	*as in*	wet /wet/

US

1 Let's /lets/

A Let's not quarrel.
B Let's keep calm.
A Let's control ourselves.
B Let's remember where we are.
A Let's remember *who** we are.
B Let's remember *what* we are.
A Hah! I know what *you* are! *You* are the most . . .
B And *you* are the most . . .
A But let's not quarrel.
B Let's *try* to keep calm.

*Words in italics should be given extra emphasis.

DO

2 D'you /dju/

A Well, now, what exactly d'you have in mind?
B What do I have in mind? Oh, yes. Yes. Well, d'you remember Partington?
A Partington . . . Partington . . . Oh, *Partington*! D'you mean the chap who . . . Hm! A dangerous man, Partington! Nasty man! Shocking!
B D'you think he could do the job for us?
A Perfectly. D'you want me to get him?

DO

3 Don't /dəʊnt/

A Don't open that, please.
B Oh.
A And please don't do that.
B Don't do what?
A That. If you don't mind.
B And this?
A Don't, please.
B Don't, don't, don't! Don't you ever say 'do'? Well, I don't want to stay here any longer! I shall leave!
A Do.

DO

4 Revise Dialogues 1–3

A I don't think I know you.
B I don't think I know *you*.
A Let's introduce ourselves.
B Let's do that.
A Smith. John Smith.
B John Smith also.
A How d'you do?
B How d'you do?

AM

5 I'm /aɪm/

A I'm lazy.
B I'm in love with you.
A I'm untidy.
B I'm in love with you.
A I'm extremely bad tempered.
B But I'm in *love* with you!
A And I'm in love with Michael.

AM

6 I'm /aɪm/ not

A I'm not saying she was foolish.
B Oh, *I'm* not saying she was foolish.
A I'm not saying she was wrong.
B Oh, no. I'm not, either.
A And I'm not saying she deserved . . . you know what!
B Oh, I'm *certainly* not saying she deserved . . . you know what!
A I'm not one of those people who spreads gossip, as you know.
B And I'm not one of those who *listens* to gossip, I can tell you.
A But even so . . .
B Yes, Elsie?

IS

7 He's /hiz/ John's /dʒɒnz/ Jack's /dʒæks/

A John's in, is he?
B He's out, actually.
A Oh, When's he expected back?
B No idea. Jack's in, though.
A Who's Jack?
B The boss.
A Surely, John's the boss. At least, he always *says* he's the boss –
and, anyway, he's the man I want to see. But you say he's out?
B He *is* out.

IS

8 She's /ʃiz/

A She's coming!
B She's coming!
A Oh, look! She's lovely! She's exquisite!
B Beautiful! She's beautiful!
A Look! She's wearing silk!
B She's wearing diamonds!
A Oh, dear! She's leaving!
B What a shame!
A How sad!
B She's *fatter* than I expected.

9 It's /ɪts/ Who's? /huz/

A   It's time! It's time to go!
B   Oh, it's only half past. Plenty of time.
A   Look, it's *awful* being late every time!
B   Who's late?
A   It's always the same! Late for everything! Late, late, late! It's ill-mannered! Discourteous!
B   Relax.
A   It's embarrassing!
B   Relax!
A   And they think it's *me*!!

10 Isn't /ˈɪznt/   It's /ɪts/ not   He's /hiz/ not

A   Wilfrid, isn't that Mr Brown?
B   Mr Brown? Here? Surely it's not Mr Brown.
A   He isn't alone, either! Look!
B   Well, that's certainly not *Mrs* Brown, is it?
A   Isn't it Miss Middleton? Well, well!
B   Good afternoon, Mr Brown.
A   Isn't it a lovely day?

ARE   **11** You're /jɔ (r)/*

A So you're Jane. Welcome.

B And you're Simon's father.

A So you're to be my daughter-in-law. Well, I must say you're *extremely* attractive. Beautiful, in fact.

B Thank you.

A But I have to confess you're just a little bit . . . well . . .

B Older than you expected?

A No, no, no, no. Er . . . did you meet my wife, by the way?

B Yes. And I must confess that . . . well . . .

A Simon's mother died, you know. I married again.

* Linking 'r' before a vowel. See *Link-up*, in this series.

12 They're /ðeə (r)/

A   Are they still there?
B   Of course they're there.
A   They're a menace! Close the window!
B   Oh, they're all right.
A   But it's three o'clock in the morning!
B   They're going, I think. Yes, they're going.
A   Good.
B   Anyway – they're married.
A   To each other?
B   Course they are. So are we.
A   They're not giving you *ideas*, I suppose?

13 We're /wɪə(r)/

A   Tell him we're here, will you?
B   We're here. We're in here.
A   Louder.
B   We're in here, Mr Bagshaw! Please come along now! We're ready for you!
A   Well, we're not going to wait all day. Where is he?
B   In *there*, I think. If you see what I mean.

14 Aren't /ɑnt/—'re not

A   You're not feeling tired, are you, dear?
B   Only my legs, love. They aren't as young as they were!
A   Well, we aren't far from the hotel now.
B   We're not doing anything tonight, are we?
A   Aren't we playing cards, dear? With the Potters?
B   Oh, yes, of course.
A   They're a splendid old couple, aren't they?
B   Splendid, yes.
A   Charming. And so dignified.
B   Even so, we're not using *their* pack of cards again tonight, *I* can tell you!

15 Revise Dialogues 5–14

A I'm looking for something rather smaller.
B How about these? They're smaller.
A Oh, yes. They're nice. That's nice, especially.
B It is, isn't it?
A But it's not *quite* what I'm seeking.
B These aren't suitable, I suppose? We're selling a lot of them, actually.
A Oh, yes. Yes, they're exactly right for *me* . . .
B Good.
A But they're for my sister, you see, and she's . . .

16 Revise Dialogues 5–14

A They're a poor team, Bill.
B They're a *terrible* team, Tony.
A The captain isn't much good.
B Hopeless. He's a hopeless captain.
A And Green. Well, he's useless, isn't he?
B Useless. There isn't a good player in the side.
A Not one. They're a complete waste of time.
B Not worth watching.
A Well, Bill, it's two o'clock. If you're ready . . .
B I'm ready, Tony. Mum! Mum! We're off to the match! Bye, Mum!

WILL **17** I'll /aɪl/ You'll /jul/

A I'll stop if you'll stop.
B If you'll stop, I'll stop, yes.
A You'll feel much better if you stop.
B Probably you'll lose your cough.
A And I'll certainly save money.
B I'll stop immediately, I think.
A Me too. I'll never have another.
B Or perhaps I'll have just *one* more.

WILL **18** He'll /hil/ She'll /ʃil/

A He'll open the gate for her.
B She'll say thank you.
A He'll walk up the path behind her.
B She'll wait for him to open the door.
A He'll look for his key.
B She'll sniff at the roses till he finds it.
A He'll say, 'Ah! Got it!'
B She'll smile.
A Here they come.
B Sh!

15

19 It'll /ɪtl/

A It'll improve soon. The others'll be coming.
B Then the fun'll begin, honestly.
A John'll be bringing his guitar.
B And Pete'll be here.
A It'll warm up soon, honestly.
B Don't go.
A Please stay.
B It'll be no fun without you.
A It'll be *hopeless* without girls.

WILL **20** We'll /wil/ You'll /jul/ They'll /ðeɪl/

A If you'll sign here, please . . .
B We'll do the rest.
A We'll arrange everything.
B We'll handle all the details.
A You'll have nothing more to worry about.
B You'll have no need to concern yourself any further.
A And those problems . . .
B Those anxieties . . .
A They'll all disappear – *dear* Mrs Parker . . .
B If you'll kindly sign here, please.
A Yes, here.

21 Won't /wəʊnt/

A He won't help us.
B He won't do anything.
A He won't cooperate.
B Why won't he help?
A Why won't he help us?
B Well, if he won't help us . . .
A If he won't, he won't.
B Right.
A But we won't forget, will we?
B We won't.

22 Revise Dialogues 17–21

A I'll tell you what'll happen.
B What'll happen?
A They'll run away.
B They won't surely!
A He'll come and fetch her, and they'll run away.
B We'll have to stop them. We have a responsibility to their parents.
A We'll do no such thing. We'll turn a blind eye.
B Harry!
A And hope they'll be happy, and never have any regrets.
B Really, Harry!
A Well, *we* are, Emily, aren't we?
B Harry, that was different – and a long time ago!
A Give us a kiss!

23 Revise Dialogues 17–21

A This'll be the last tune.

B I *hope* it'll be the last tune.

A It's one o'clock. They'll finish after this. I'll telephone the manager if they don't.

B We'll *never* get any sleep!

A Just *listen* to that noise!

B D'you think they'll be having another dance tomorrow night?

A Well, if they do . . .

B Oh, if they do . . .

A We'll complain.

B We will.

A Or shall we go to it?

HAVE   **24** I've /aɪv/   You've /juv/

A   I've got something for you.
B   You've got something for me?
A   Well, open it.
B   A birthday present for me? Now what can it be?
A   Like it?
B   Thank you, darling. Just what I've always wanted. How did you guess?
A   Darling, I've been thinking.
B   Mm?
A   You've got *so* many pipes now. How about a change next year?

HAVE   **25** They've /ðeɪv/   We've /wiv/

A   We've failed.
B   We've failed? Both of us?
A   They've passed.
B   They've passed? All of them?
A   They've all passed except us.
B   But if they've passed, how have we failed?
A   Well, we *have*. I've seen the list.
B   But we've planned a celebration!
A   Forget it.
B   We've bought all those bottles!
A   Well, get them out, then.

HAVE   **26** Haven't /hævnt/—'ve not

A   I haven't always lived in this cottage, you know.
B   Haven't you? How pretty it is!
A   You've not been here long, of course.
B   I haven't, no. Only a month, in fact. But it's a very nice village. I've grown to love it already.
A   You haven't seen Ferringly House, yet, I suppose?
B   Oh, it's magnificent! A beautiful house!
A   But the *new* people haven't looked after it properly, you know.
B   Well, I haven't seen it closely, of course, Mrs, er . . .
A   Ferringly. Madeleine Ferringly.

HAVE   **27** He's /hiz/   She's /ʃiz/   It's /ɪts/

A Jim's left, of course.
B He's left, too, has he?
A And Jean.
B Yes, she's gone to work at Fletcher's, they tell me.
A Oh, it's changed a lot since you were here. It's become much more
   efficient, of course. But it's lost the personal touch, I'm afraid.
B And what about our old friend Martin?
A Oh, Martin's stayed on.
B And become more efficient?
A He's had to. At avoiding work, that is.

HAVE   **28** Hasn't /ˈhæznt/

A Hasn't the doctor come yet?
B No. The doctor hasn't been called.
A But this is urgent!
B Grandfather hasn't seen a doctor for sixty years.
   He's stubborn.
A Well tell him he *must*. He hasn't any choice.
B All right. But . . .
A And tell him Dr Fenton's a very good-looking young woman.

29   Revise Dialogues 24–28

A   I've given twenty.
B   And I've given ten.
A   And Uncle Mike – he's given fifty. And Auntie Agnes . . .
B   She's given twenty-five.
A   Everyone's given something.
B   So we've *nearly* reached our target.
A   And we *know* you've contributed once already, Dad . . .
B   But Daddy, could you . . .

30   Revise Dialogues 24–28

A   He's got a crooked nose.
B   She's got skinny arms.
A   He hasn't shaved.
B   She's forgotten to comb her hair.
A   He's got a very poor job.
B   She hasn't got a job at *all*.
A   They've never had much money.
B   And whenever they've had some, they've spent it.
A   But they've always been happy.
B   Exceptionally happy.
A   That couple in the mirror.
B   That funny looking pair.

A   It's gone. It's not here.
B   It's not there? Ask Vic where he's put it!
A   Vic's gone.
B   He's gone? Where's he gone?
A   Nobody knows where he's gone.
B   Well, get Sheila.
A   Hm!
B   Sheila too? But that's incredible!
A   Is it?

A   It's stopping outside her house.
B   It's stopped.
A   Who's inside?
B   It's a man.
A   It's a fine car. It's old. But it's been *very* well maintained.
B   He's going to the door. He's very distinguished.
A   He's ringing again. She's coming. She's a beautiful old lady, you know.
B   And *very* well maintained.

      * —'s pronounced: /s/ after a voiceless sound, e.g. it's /s/;
                         /z/ after a voiced sound, e.g. he's /z/.

HAD

33 He'd /hid/   You'd /jud/

A He'd already gone when I got there.
B I wish you'd spoken to him.
A You really think he'd have helped?
B I think he'd have tried. I wish you'd seen him.
A Anyway, he'd left, as I say. He'd left early, actually.
B Oh.
A Perhaps he'd been told I was coming!

HAD

34 I'd /aɪd/   She'd /ʃid/

A She mustn't blame herself, of course. But if she'd asked someone . . .
B Or if *I'd* asked someone . . .
A If she'd been alert . . .
B If *I'd* been alert . . .
A If only she'd *checked* carefully!
B If only *I'd* checked carefully!
A Oh, well. Never mind.
B Hm!
A We mustn't blame ourselves.

HAD   **35** It'd /ɪtəd/

A Then we realised it'd escaped.

B It'd bitten through one of the bars and squeezed through the gap . . .

A And before it ran away . . .

B It'd been in the kitchen . . .

A It'd knocked everything over . . .

B Broken a dish, smashed a plate . . .

A And it'd eaten my supper!

B Anyway, thank you for bringing it back.

A We were afraid it'd been killed.

B And we missed it, *terribly*!

HAD

36 We'd /wid/   You'd /jud/   They'd /ðeɪd/

A Tim, I told you we'd met the Frasers, didn't I?
B Well, Tim, they told us they'd seen you.
A They'd just got out of their car, they said . . .
B When they saw you running down to the beach . . .
A With Jane.
B We didn't say anything, of course.
A But why did you tell us you'd been in town all day?
B With Frieda?

HAD

37 —'d /d/   Hadn't /ˈhædnt/

A He hadn't got time for a drink, he said . . .
B But when he'd drunk it . . .
A He said he hadn't got time for a meal . . .
B But when he'd eaten it . . .
A He said he hadn't come to stay the night . . .
B And when he'd stayed a week . . .
A He stayed another . . .
B And another . . .
A And hoped he hadn't outstayed his welcome.
B So, as I say – we'd *hoped* to let you have the spare room . . .
A If *he* hadn't come, and if . . . oh . . . er . . . hullo!
B Had a good day?

A I hadn't seen him for many many years.

B And when you met him that day?

A Oh, he'd changed terribly.

B He'd changed? How?

A Not his age, of course. I'd expected that.

B His attitudes? His beliefs?

A He'd become another person. Everything he'd believed in, in the old days, seemed to mean nothing to him any more – all the ideals we'd shared! It was *so* disappointing!

B Indeed, yes.

A However – you say your magazine's offered ten thousand for the full story. Now, if they'd offered me *twenty* . . .

WOULD   **39** I'd /aɪd/ You'd /jud/ She'd /ʃid/ He'd /hid/

A   If you'd like to know what I'd like, I'd like a car.
B   She'd like a car, if you'd like to know.
A   I'd *adore* some diamonds!
B   She'd *adore* some diamonds!
A   And I'd *love* a mink coat!
B   Oh, she'd *love* a mink coat!
A   But if that's too expensive . . .
B   She'd like a hamburger.
A   Oh, all right. I'll pay. One hamburger, please.
B   Make it three.

WOULD   **40** It'd /ɪtəd/

A   It'd be difficult to tell him, of course.
B   It'd obviously come as a shock.
A   It'd seem a bit harsh, I suppose.
B   Yes, I suppose it would.
A   And in a way, it'd be lonely without him.
B   Oh, it'd be quieter, no doubt.
A   But it'd be best to tell him.
B   Yes.
A   It'd be best if *you* told him.

WOULD   **41** We'd /wid/ They'd /ðeɪd/

A   It's a lovely house.
B   Yes. And if they'd paint it . . .
A   If they'd put in new windows . . .
B   And they'd repair the roof . . .
A   And build us a new garage . . .
B   And modernise the kitchen . . .
A   We'd buy it, of course.
B   Well, we'd *think* about it, certainly.
A   Yes.
B   If they'd bring down the price.

42 Wouldn't /ˈwʊdnt/

A   Well?
B   Well, they said they wouldn't paint it.
A   Wouldn't they put in new windows?
B   They wouldn't. Or repair the roof.
A   Or build a garage? Or modernise the kitchen?
B   No.
A   And the price?
B   They wouldn't lower it at all.
A   So you told them we wouldn't be interested, of course.
B   I told them we'd think about it.
A   Mm. Oh, dear. It's a lovely house, isn't it?
B   Mm. It wouldn't be a *bargain*, of course. But . . .

43   Revise Dialogues 39–42

A   If he'd known . . .
B   He'd have told the police.
A   And if he'd told the police?
B   They'd be here now.
A   But, of course, I wouldn't do a silly thing like that, would I?
     It'd spoil my plans.
B   What plans?
A   *My* plans.
B   *What* plans?
A   My plans for *him*.
B   Oh.
A   And my plans for *you* – my dear.

44 —'d /d/

A I knew you'd come.
B You knew I *had* come? Or I *would* come?
A Oh – *had* come, sorry. I was sure you *would* come, some time.
B Well, how did you *know* I'd come?
A I knew you'd come because I saw your car.
B No, sorry – I mean how did you know I *would* come?
A Well, it's obvious, isn't it? I'd told you Betty'd be here!

45 Hadn't /hædnt/ Wouldn't /wʊdnt/

A I hadn't expected a promotion.
B Well, you wouldn't, would you?
A I really hadn't expected it.
B You wouldn't, I suppose.
A I certainly wouldn't have got it if he'd checked my file.
B Oh, he checked it, certainly – because *I* gave it to him.
A But surely, if he'd seen that old letter, he wouldn't have promoted me.
B If he'd seen it, he wouldn't, no.
A Naughty girl.

MODALS + HAVE   **46**   Should've /ˈʃʊdəv/etc.

A   You should've stopped him!
B   *You* should've stopped him!
A   Surely you must've seen what was going on!
B   Well, *you* must've seen, too, mustn't you?
A   He must've left the country by now!
B   Anyway, what about Mr Binns? *He* could've stopped him!
A   Yes, now that I think about it, he could – easily. He *could've*
     stopped him.
B   He *should've* stopped him.
A   Where *is* Mr Binns, by the way?

MODALS + HAVE   **47**   Could've /ˈkʊdəv/etc.

A   But, darling, if only you could've apologised!
B   Hm! *He* should've apologised to *me!*
A   But he's *older* than you. You could've said you were sorry,
     surely.
B   I suppose I could've *said* I was. But that would've been telling a lie.
A   But only a *little* one. You could've said it, just to keep the
     peace. For *my* sake!
B   Oh, all right. You win. Where is the old devil?

48 General Revision

A Now, let's look at it. D'you think it'll do?
B I don't, no.
A I must say, I'm rather pleased with it.
B Well I'm not! He's a crook, that man.
A Not so loud! He's coming back.
B Antique, indeed!
A Sh!
B He's probably made it himself.
A Ah, Mr Bell! Well, now, we've looked at it, and we . . .

49 General Revision

A Oh, no, we're not at all excited, are we?
B We're absolutely calm, aren't we?
A We've always said we'd take it calmly, haven't we?
B We wouldn't get excited, we said.
A And we haven't, have we?
B After all, it's a perfectly ordinary event, isn't it?
A It'd be silly not to take it coolly.
B Indeed, yes.
A Yes.
B WHOOPEEEEEEEEEEEEEEEEEEEEEEEEEEEE!!!!!!!!!!!!!!!
A Ha ha ha ha ha ha ha! He he he he he he!
B HO ho ho ho ho ho ho ho ho ho ho ho ho! HA ha ha. . . .

50 Conclusion

A   Well, that's the end of 'Contractions'.
B   Mm.*
A   Hope you've enjoyed it.
B   Mm.
A   Hope it's helped you.
B   Mm.
A   Hope we'll meet again some time.
B   Mm.

* On the tape, Speaker B's part is not recorded. Students should supply their own intonation on 'Mm' according to which of the many possible meanings they wish to convey.